# The Last Munro

A Play

Dave Watson

A Samuel French Acting Edition

SAMUEL FRENCH

FOUNDED 1830

SAMUELFRENCH-LONDON.CO.UK
SAMUELFRENCH.COM

*THE LAST MUNRO* is fully protected under the copyright laws of the British Commonwealth, including Canada, the United States of America, and all other countries of the Copyright Union. All rights, including professional and amateur stage productions, recitation, lecturing, public reading, motion picture, radio broadcasting, television and the rights of translation into foreign languages are strictly reserved.

ISBN 978-0-573-12147-0

www.samuelfrench-london.co.uk

www.samuelfrench.com



CAUTION: Professional and amateur producers are hereby warned that *THE LAST MUNRO* is subject to a licensing fee. Publication of this play does not imply availability for performance. Both amateurs and professionals considering a production are strongly advised to apply to the appropriate agent before starting rehearsals, advertising, or booking a theatre. A licensing fee must be paid whether the title is presented for charity or gain and whether or not admission is charged.

The professional rights in this play are controlled by Samuel French Ltd, 52 Fitzroy Street, London, W1T 5JR.

## CHARACTERS

**Mark**, *20s*
**Sandra**, *20s*
**John**, *late middle-age*


The action of the play takes place on the summit of Stob Dearg on the Buachaille Etive Mor, Scotland, in early summer

Time — the present


## PRONUNCIATION NOTES

| | |
|---|---|
| Stob Dearg | Stop Jerrack |
| Buachaille Etive Mor | Booachill Etiv Moar |
| Creise | Kraysh |
| Meall a'Bhuiridh | Myowl a Vooree |
| Sgurr Mhic Choinnich | Skoor Veechk Chunyeech |
| Schiehallion | Shee-hallian |

# THE LAST MUNRO

*The summit of Stob Dearg on the Buachaille Etive Mor, Scotland.
Early summer*

*A stone cairn marks the mountain's peak*

*Mark enters, carrying a rucksack. He is a fit, middle-class, nouveau
sportsman in his twenties, from the city*

**Mark** (*shouting off and down*)  Come on, Sandra! You've nearly
  made it! (*He moves to the cairn, smacks the top of it and looks
  round triumphantly*) Number fifty-three! (*He takes off his rucksack and leans it against the cairn, then goes back to view
  Sandra's progress. Shouting off and down*) Come on, darling!
**Sandra** (*off; below*) Piss off!

*Mark smiles and shakes his head. He tours the mountain top, then
returns to watch Sandra's approach*

**Mark**  (*calling*) For God's sake, Sandra! You've only got twenty
  metres to go!
**Sandra** (*off*)  My feet hurt!
**Mark**  You can't stop there! This is the top!
**Sandra** (*off*)  You said that back down there, Mark!
**Mark**  I know. I lied. It was the mist. But this *is* the top!
**Sandra** (*off*)  Mark, I don't bloody well believe you!
**Mark**  It is, honestly! Come on, Sandra! Just a little further!
**Sandra** (*off*)  Bugger off!
**Mark**  Please yourself! Just remember I've got all the food. (*He
  returns to the cairn. Sighing*) Bloody women. (*He sits and opens
  the rucksack*)

*There is a pause*

*Sandra enters, struggling. She is Mark's wife, a pretty, image-conscious woman, in her twenties*

**Sandra**  Well, thank you! Thanks a bloody bunch!

**Mark** (*laughing*)  What's the matter?

**Sandra**  You could have damn well waited! I might have got lost in that ruddy fog.

**Mark**  Oh, come on. It's only a little light mist. It'll soon clear. Anyway, you've made it.

**Sandra**  No thanks to you! (*She collapses on to a rock*) Jesus! I'm going to die! Dead from exhaustion and exposure, my make-up smeared with sweat and my hair looking like a gorse bush.

**Mark** (*taking a flask from his rucksack; laughing*)  Have some coffee.

**Sandra**  And does my sadist of a husband care? Does he hell!

**Mark**  Come on. It's not that bad.

**Sandra**  And you know the worst bit? *I* don't damn well care! I have passed the pain barrier, the discomfort barrier, the I-look-a-bloody-mess barrier. I can only lie on this rocky peak of purgatory ready to expiate my venial sins. God! I must have committed quite a few to deserve this!

**Mark** (*laughing*)  You'll feel better when you've eaten. (*He pours himself a coffee*) Do you want coffee?

**Sandra**  No. I want a helicopter or two strong hairy men from the mountain rescue with a stretcher! Oh, my feet! (*She unlaces her boot and pulls it off*)

**Mark**  Have you got a blister?

**Sandra** (*pulling off her sock and inspecting her foot*) Mark, darling, blisters, plural! I've got blisters on my blisters. I'll probably walk with a limp for the rest of my life. Look at that!

**Mark**  Here. I've got some plasters. (*He searches in his rucksack pocket and finds some plasters*) I did warn you.

**Sandra**  The Torquemada Climbing Club. Jesus! (*She takes the plasters from Mark and applies one to her foot during the following*)

**Mark** (*taking out a book and pencil and putting a tick on a list*)
That's fifty-three.
**Sandra** Just look at my feet.
**Mark** Fifty-three. Don't you think that's good?
**Sandra** My hero! (*She looks around*) So this is it?
**Mark** Don't you think it was worth it? Your first Munro.
**Sandra** Wonderful. "From scenes like these auld Scotia's grandeur
springs." Now, get me a sandwich. (*She pulls her boot back on*)

*During the following Mark searches in the rucksack with increasing
consternation, finally pulling all the contents out. There is a
considerable amount of Sandra's clothing in the rucksack*

What is this called? The Buckle whatsit?
**Mark** (*sighing*) Buachaille Etive Mor. I told you. It means the big
herdsman of Etive. That, in case you didn't know, is Glen Etive
down there.
**Sandra** Oh, forgive me for asking. Anyway, how can you tell? I
can't see anything. It might as well be Sauchiehall Street with all
that fog. You're certain this is the top?
**Mark** The Buachaille Etive Mor is the name of the whole thing.
**Sandra** But this is the top?
**Mark** Yes. This is the highest point: Stob Dearg, the red peak.
Didn't you notice the pinkness of the stone?
**Sandra** You should have warned me. I'd have worn something
different to match the rocks. Hurry up with the sarnies. I'm
starving.
**Mark** To do the whole of the Buachaille, we carry on round the
ridge over two other tops to Stob na Brioge.
**Sandra** Pardon me?
**Mark** Stob na Brioge. Look, it's above the mist.
**Sandra** No, darling, no. That little bit you slipped in — the bit about
*we* carry on ...
**Mark** What?
**Sandra** You said *we* carry on.
**Mark** Uhuh. It's just a simple ridge walk. Round to the other tops
and then down the way we came up.

**Sandra**  You said *this* was the top.

**Mark**  So it is.

**Sandra**  But if this is the top and that is a top and there are two other
tops in between ... ?

**Mark**  Yes?

**Sandra**  Then which *is* the ruddy top?

**Mark**  Ah, no. I thought I'd explained. This, Stob Dearg, is the
summit. This is designated as a mountain, the Munro, whereas
those three peaks are tops because they don't have a clear ascent
of two hundred and fifty feet on all sides.

**Sandra**  Right. If you say so. So, as well as this, you intend us to
climb three other tops?

**Mark**  She's got it! By George, she's got it!

**Sandra**  I may be thick, but explain to my why we have to prolong
this excruciating agony, by hobbling another fifty miles over
treacherous bloody rock — sorry, treacherous bloody pink rock!

**Mark**  Don't exaggerate. It's not as far as it looks.

**Sandra**  It looks plenty far to me!

**Mark**  You want to do the whole mountain, don't you?

**Sandra**  In a word, Mark, no. This may come as a great shock to you.
What I *want* to be doing is sitting in front of the pub fire reading
the Sunday paper.

**Mark**  We can't just shoot up here, tick it off and shoot back down.

**Sandra**  Why not? I thought that's what Munro bagging was all
about.

**Mark**  No, no. There's got to be more to it than that. You have to
explore the whole character of the hill.

**Sandra**  Oh, yes.

**Mark**  Actually, I thought we might slip down into the Lairig
Gartain and pop up the Buachaille Etive Beag.

**Sandra**  Uhuh. Slip down. Pop up? Why not?

**Mark**  That would be two Munros in a day.

**Sandra**  Yes. I'll have two and you'll have ... fifty-four.

**Mark**  (*encouraged*)  That's right. D'you fancy it?

**Sandra**  Mark, you must be damn well joking! You can slip down
and pop up whatever you like. I'm going to slip right down the
way we came up and pop into the bloody bar for a stiff whisky.
Or three!

**Mark** Oh, come on. It's the Little Herdsman of Etive.

**Sandra** I don't care if it's the Medium-sized Herdsman of Milngavie! I'm going straight back down, buddy. And before this mist gets any thicker.

**Mark** Oh, come on, Sandra.

**Sandra** Don't "Oh, come on, Sandra" me. I mean it, Mark. I'm not going a step further than absolutely necessary. Now give me a blooming sandwich.

**Mark** Uh, bad news, there, I'm afraid.

**Sandra** What do you mean?

**Mark** We — uh — we seem to have forgotten them.

**Sandra** We seem to have what? You are joking? Tell me you're joking!

**Mark** Sorry. We must have left them on the kitchen table.

**Sandra** Oh, bloody great! That's tremendous! And what is this "we" business? You, the great experienced man of the mountains — you're the one that said "Leave it all to me." You're the one that packed the rucksack. There's no "*we*" involved.

**Mark** All right, all right. So *I* forgot the sandwiches. It's not the end of the world. I said sorry.

**Sandra** That's all right then. I may possibly die of exposure and malnutrition, but your apology will make me bear it all with happy fortitude. Jesus! Isn't there anything to eat? (*She searches through the contents of the rucksack. She finds a small tin and opens it*) What's in here?

**Mark** That's my survival tin.

**Sandra** Wonderful. Bloody wonderful! We have no food, but we do have (*she reads the inventory*) one wire saw, one button compass — liquid filled, no less — one fishing kit, potassium permanganate, one sewing pack. One reflecting mirror, matches (twenty), water purification tablets (twelve). A candle, oh, yum, yum! One firelighting flint with steel, one pencil, oh, and a waterproof instruction leaflet with Morse code directions. We may not have any sandwiches. But who cares, as long as we remembered this most *essential* of kit!

**Mark** Oh, give us a break, Sandra.

**Sandra** I'll tell you what. You start fishing while I heliograph the Kingshouse Hotel for a three course lunch to be sent up. Or perhaps you'd rather get out your sewing pack and practice your petit-bloody-point! (*She tosses the tin back with disgust*)

**Mark**  I said I was sorry.

**Sandra**  Tread carefully, Mark. No words can adequately express the black rage I feel inside me. I could kill!

**Mark**  Calm down, for goodness sake. Here. (*He produces a tube of Polos*) Have a Polo.

**Sandra**  A Polo? A Polo? Mark, last night I prepared, cut and wrapped a packet of carefully considered sandwiches, filled variously with cold smoked meat — pastrami, Parma ham and thin corned beef with mustard — a mild vegetarian cheddar and a compote of fruits of the hedgerow. Thanks to you, they are now sitting in the middle of the kitchen table. I cannot believe you have the gall to offer me, as a substitute, a crappy bloody mint!

**Mark**  For Christ's sake, stop wingeing. It's no wonder I forgot with all the bloody fuss you made this morning.

**Sandra**  Fuss? What fuss?

**Mark** (*mimicking her*) Oh, my God, look at my hair. Should I wear the Icelandic woollen hat or a hard scarf? No perhaps a headband. What about a jumper — the blue cashmere or the red Benetton? The multi-coloured leggings or the lightweight action trousers? What a problem! I know! I'll put everything into Mark's rucksack and he can lug the whole frigging lot up the mountain. That way, should I be improperly attired for a chance social function *en route*, I can nip behind a boulder and change into something suitable.

**Sandra**  Oh, very droll.

**Mark**  It's not a rucksack I need with you. It's a damned chest of drawers!

**Sandra**  At least I left my potassium permanganate and firelighting flint at home.

**Mark**  It's no surprise that I forgot the sandwiches. With your comprehensive sports wardrobe, there's no bloody room for them!

**Sandra**  Oh! (*She turns away angrily*)

*There is a pause*

I suppose there's no chocolate or crisps? No, we ate them, didn't we?

**Mark**  *You* ate them, you mean. You scoffed them all before we even got out of the car.

**Sandra**  I was hungry. I didn't have any breakfast.

**Mark**  Well, if you hadn't spent so long putting on your bloody make-up, you might have had time for some.

**Sandra**  I can't go without make-up. I feel undressed.

**Mark**  Sandra, look around. There is no-one for bloody miles. It's a funny thing about sheep. They just don't care if you're wearing lipstick or not.

*He makes to stuff the rucksack contents back but spots something in the bottom. He withdraws a very squashed Mars bar from the rucksack*

**Mark**  There's a Mars bar.

**Sandra**  (*full of hope*)  What?

**Mark**  A Mars bar. It's a bit squashed.

**Sandra**  Ye gods! That's disgusting. How many years has that been festering at the bottom of your sack? Look at it! That has been nestling unnoticed for God knows how long, cheek by jowl with your sodden, sweaty clothing — not to mention the other unthinkable items of decomposing detritus that might be lurking down there.

**Mark**  I take it you don't want it, then?

**Sandra**  Oh, get real! I suppose there's none of those cartons of orange left?

**Mark**  You drank them all on the way up.

**Sandra**  I was thirsty.

**Mark**  No wonder. After the crisps and chocolate.

**Sandra**  Oh, shut up. Give me some coffee.

*Mark pours out a cup of coffee and hands it to Sandra*

At least I won't die of thirst. (*She drinks, then spits the coffee back into the cup*) Mark! This has got sugar in it! You know I can't drink coffee with sugar!

**Mark**  Sorry. I forgot. I didn't think. Force of habit. I'm used to being on my own.

**Sandra**  Hold that thought! Mark, this is a nightmare! (*She gets up and stamps away angrily*) A nightmare heading straight towards divorce: do not pass "Go", do not collect two hundred pounds!

**Mark**  (*unwrapping the Mars bar*) Sure you don't want a bit of this?

**Sandra**  Mark. Any minute now I'm going to hurl myself off this mountain top.

**Mark**  (*chewing the Mars bar*) It's not that bad, you know.

*Sandra screams in frustration. She pauses. She comes morosely back to Mark*

Feeling better?

**Sandra**  Don't talk to me.

**Mark**  Come on. We'll laugh about this tomorrow.

**Sandra**  (*grimly*)  I told you not to talk to me!

**Mark**  We'll go straight down when the mist clears a little. We'll forget Stob na Brioge.

**Sandra**  Damned right, we will. My God! Whatever possessed me to do this?

**Mark**  I did warn you. Try something easy first, I said. But oh, no. Mrs "Anything-you-can-do, we're-as-good-as-you-bloody-men" has to go for a big one right away.

**Sandra**  Oh, shut up, you smug bastard!

**Mark**  Fine. Fine. That's what I call a considered and well-argued response.

**Sandra**  What do you expect? Oscar Wilde? This isn't what you said it would be like. You forgot to mention the quagmire down there, the bloody great boulders, the sheep, the midges, the flies, to say nothing of this damned mist which has rendered the whole torment invisible!

**Mark**  You were the one that demanded to come. (*He mimics Sandra*) Take me with you, Mark. I want to share your interests. I want to be part of everything you do. I knew it was a mistake to bring you. God, you moaned and bitched the whole way up.

**Sandra**  So sorry! So sorry to be such a burden to you. I won't say
  another word.
**Mark**  That'll be the day.
**Sandra**  Not another complaint will pass my lips.

*There is a pause. Sandra walks about, trying to contain her
discomfort. She can finally bear it no longer*

  God, now I'm getting cold! (*She stands on the edge of the peak
  and flaps her arms to keep warm. She suddenly freezes mid-flap
  and gives a start of alarm*) Mark! Mark! There's a bloody great
  animal coming at us through the mist. (*She runs to Mark for
  protection*) That just puts the tin lid on it!  The abominable
  snowman!

*John enters. He is an experienced climber in late middle age,
unhurried and deliberate. He carries a rucksack and a small
stone*

**John**  Afternoon.
**Mark**  Hi.
**Sandra**  Hallo.

*John carefully puts the small stone at the base of the cairn. He stands
back solemnly. His ritual completed, he turns to the others*

**John**  Pity about the mist. I was looking forward to the view.
**Sandra**  Tell us about it.
**Mark**  Do you think it will clear soon?
**John** (*looking round*) The wind has moved. (*He nods*) Ay. I expect
  it will clear shortly. (*He takes his rucksack off and sits a little way
  from Mark and Sandra*) You'll have come up from Altnafeath?
**Mark**  Uhuh. You too?

*John nods and takes a flask from his rucksack. He pours himself a
cup of soup*

**Sandra** (*to Mark*)  I'm putting on another jumper. (*She does so. Suddenly she spots John's soup*) I'm damn well freezing now. (*Aside, to Mark*) Mark! He's got soup!

**Mark**  For goodness sake, Sandra.

**Sandra**  Looks like Scotch broth.

**Mark**  Shh!

**Sandra**  God, I could kill for some of that. Mark! Let's mug him!

**Mark**  Sandra, behave yourself.

**Sandra**  Go on. Ask him for some.

**Mark**  Get lost. Will I hell!

**Sandra**  Go on. It's a ruddy great flask. He can't want all of that.

**Mark**  Sandra, don't be ridiculous.

**Sandra**  Well, I will. (*She circles John nonchalantly*) This dashed mist, eh?

**John**  It'll clear soon. Look. There's Creise and Meall a'Bhuiridh.

**Sandra**  Oh, yes. I'd recognise them anywhere. Still a little chilly.

**John**  Ay. But the soup fair warms you up. (*He drinks with relish*)

**Sandra**  Mm. Looks good. Home made?

**John**  Ay. (*He drinks again*)

**Sandra**  Are you — going on to the other *tops*?

**John**  I'll see. These old legs aren't what they used to be.

**Sandra**  That — soup of yours will soon put you right.

**John**  Ay. It will that. (*He drinks again*) Sorry. Would you like some?

**Sandra**  What? Oh, no. Thanks.

**John**  No, really. Go on. There's far too much for me.

**Sandra**  No, no. I couldn't ... well ... if you've ... a drop to spare.

**John**  Of course, lass. Here.

*John pours a cup of soup and hands it to Sandra*

What about your man?

**Sandra**  No, he's all right. He's got a Mars bar. (*She drinks with relish*) That's very kind of you. Oh, this is wonderful. Your wife must be a great cook.

**Mark**  I see you had the good sense to leave her at home.

**John** (*laughing*)  No, no. I made this myself.
**Sandra**  It's brilliant.
**John**  Have some more. Give some to the lad.

*John hands Sandra the flask*

It's far too much for me. I always make enough for two. Old habits
die hard.
**Sandra**  (*pouring more soup for them*) Your wife usually climbs
with you?
**John**  She used to.
**Sandra**  Don't tell me you forgot the sandwiches too?
**John**  Pardon me?
**Sandra**  Sorry, nothing. Just a private dig at Mr Memory over there.
He only left all the food at home. I intend to make him suffer for
this, till death do us part.
**John** (*laughing*)  I see. No. My wife ... Eileen, she died two years
ago.
**Sandra**  Oh no! Oh Hell! I can't believe what I just said! Oh, Jeez,
I'm sorry.
**John** (*laughing*)  It's OK.
**Mark** (*aside, to Sandra*)  Sandra. For God's sake, shut up. You're
a bloody embarrassment!

*Sandra gives the flask back to John*

**Sandra**  Thanks. Look, sorry. I put my big foot in it again.
**Mark** (*to Sandra*)  You put both of them in it. (*To John*) My wife's
mouth is totally independent of her brain.
**John** (*laughing*)  It's OK, lass. Really. Forget it. My name's John,
by the way.
**Sandra**  I'm Sandra. The idiot who dragged me up here and put
sugar in my coffee is Mark, my sub-normal husband.

*John laughs and produces some sandwiches from his rucksack. He
hands them to Sandra*

**John**  Here, have these. They're nothing fancy.

**Sandra**  John, you're a saint. You don't have a little keg of brandy round your neck by any chance?

**John** (*laughing*)  Sorry. Tell me, Sandra. Do you two climb a lot together?

**Sandra**  Ha! Are you kidding? Not blooming likely. He's the Munro bagger. I think I said that right.

**Mark** (*joining the others; proudly*)  Fifty-three including this. Only ... two hundred and twenty-four to go.

**Sandra**  This, John, is my first Munro ... and quite definitely my last. (*She munches a sandwich*)

**John**  I see. That bad, was it?

**Sandra**  Don't ask. How about you? You look like a seasoned campaigner.

**John**  I suppose I am. (*He laughs*) You know, this is quite a coincidence.

**Sandra**  What is?

**John**  This is your first Munro — and my last.

**Sandra**  You mean you're giving it up?

**John**  No, no. I mean I've done them all now.

**Mark**  You're kidding!

**John**  No. This is my final one.

**Sandra**  You've done them all? Every peak in Scotland over three thousand feet? Every Munro?

**John**  Every one. The Buachaille is my last.

**Sandra**  Bloody Nora! Why aren't you celebrating, John? Aren't you supposed to have a piper? A party? It's champagne you should be drinking, not soup.

**John**  Och, I'm not a great one for drinking. I am celebrating though, I suppose. But quiet like.

**Mark**  So how does it feel? To have done them all?

**John**  Oh, it's good, right enough. Funny thing is, though, there's a certain sadness in finishing. Like everything's behind you. I suppose it doesn't mean quite the same without my Eileen. You know?

**Sandra**  Oh, John, what a shame. She ... ah ... climbed them all with you?

**John**  All but twelve. We did all the rest together.

**Mark**  That's two hundred and sixty five.

**Sandra**  My husband the accountant. I wonder he didn't bring his lap-top computer with him.

**Mark**  Listen to Mrs Bonnington — the one climb to her credit.

**Sandra**  See what I have to put up with, John? If you're anything like him (*she indicates Mark*) your wife must have been quite a woman.

**John** (*laughing*) Ay, she was that. And we had a great time together — Torridon, the Fannichs, Skye. (*He laughs*) What a laugh we had on Sgurr Mhic Choinnich.

**Mark**  The Inaccessible Pinnacle?

**John**  Ay, the In Pin. I had to lower her down like a sack of tatties. She was screaming fit to bust.

**Sandra**  I bet. I've seen photos of that bloody thing. (*She has a sudden horrid thought*) God! She didn't ... you know ... ? (*She mimes a diving motion*) She wasn't ... ? Not an accident?

**John** (*laughing*)  No, no. It was her heart, poor thing. She died in hospital — though, knowing her, she'd have preferred to go up here.

*There is a pause; they are all thoughtful*

*Mark rises and looks around. He walks away to scan the view*

**Mark**  The mist is definitely clearing.

**Sandra**  Tell me something, John. I've never done this sort of thing before, I've never seen the logic ——

**John**  And you obviously haven't enjoyed it much.

**Sandra**  How did you guess? I've hated every bloody minute! You know, I can torture myself in the comfort of my own home. Tell me the truth. Did your Eileen always like climbing? God, she must have, to have done two hundred and sixty.

**John** (*laughing*)  Listen. I remember our very first climb together. It was Ben Vorlich above Loch Sloy. It seemed a grand day when we started, but as we neared the summit the wind was howling a gale. We could hardly stand upright in it. She was terrified. She wanted to go back, but I wouldn't let her. The wind blew her hat away and she couldn't see with her hair in her eyes. I was shouting, she was crying. God, it was awful.

**Sandra** But you got to the top.

**John** (*laughing*) Oh, ay. I dragged her there — eventually.

**Sandra** Typical man.

**John** Just so. Heaven knows how I managed to talk her into going again.

**Sandra** But you did.

**John** Look, Sandra. Take my advice. Stick with it. Eileen managed. You've got a good man there. By the time you've climbed even just a few mountains, the logic of hill walking will start to overtake you. By the time you've climbed a hundred, you'll know Scotland and yourselves from a brand new vantage point.

**Sandra** I suppose so.

**John** I can see you're not convinced. Don't get me wrong. Not every climb will be an enjoyable experience. Life's not like that. But every single hill has its own secrets, its own mysteries. And above you is always the possibility of a sudden revelation ...

**Mark** Wow! That's a bit too heavy for me!

**John** Ach. Only because I'm trying to put it into words. Eileen was better at it. An epiphany was what she called it. That's what she looked for. The bones of the gods that formed our wonderful land. (*He laughs*) She could be a bit poetic at times.

**Mark** (*coming back to the others*) It's definitely clearing. You can see down into Rannoch Moor.

**Sandra** Mark, why don't you go and play with your liquid-filled button compass? John and I are talking.

**Mark** I do so beg your pardon. Look out, John, she's only after your orange. Any minute now she'll split your head open with a rock and make off with your KitKat.

**Sandra** Very funny. My husband imagines he's a comedian.

**Mark** To think I came up here for peace and quiet.

**John** (*laughing*) Give her a chance. It's her first Munro.

**Mark** True. (*He shakes his head*) And you've climbed them all. All two hundred and seventy-seven.

**Sandra** (*to Mark*) Makes your fifty-three seem rather piffling, darling.

**John**  Ay. But you know, Mark, it's not such a big thing. I started like you, collecting hills like scalps, straight up and down, with hardly a sideways glance. But you'll change. At least I hope you do.

**Mark**  Change? How?

**John**  Take Beinn an Lochain at the top of the Rest and Be Thankful. Now at one time it was classified as a Munro. Then, some years ago, they re-measured it and decided it wasn't a Munro after all. Are you going to ignore a lovely hill with a wonderful view simply because it's a few feet short of the magic three thousand feet?

**Mark**  I see what you mean. (*He walks thoughtfully to the edge*)

**Sandra**  Look what you've done now, John. You've started him thinking. That's always dangerous.

**John** (*laughs*) Wheest. He's a good lad.

**Sandra**  Mm. Tell me more about Eileen, John. She must have been quite a lady.

**John**  Ay. Quite a lady.

**Sandra**  So she got to like climbing?

**John**  Once she got going, she was better at it than me — keener, fitter, faster. She used to drag me out in all weathers. A real four-season climber, she was. Ice axe, crampons, the lot.

**Sandra**  And you think I should be like her?

**John**  Why not? You could do much worse. Believe me, the mountains are twice the experience when you can share them with a companion that you love. And you have all these hills before you, still unclimbed. All those peaks shimmering blue and gold and silver on the far horizon.

**Sandra** (*looking round, inspired*) John. You're a bloody inspiration!

**John** (*laughing*) I'm glad. It's grand to see you right at the start of it. Me, I can only look back now. (*He pats a rock*) The Buachaille Etive. We both chose this hill to be our last Munro. We left this one for last. Eileen loved to see it coming up from Loch Ba and into the glen. So grand and imposing. Walls, gullies and buttresses — everything a mountain should be.

**Sandra**  God, that's so sad. She never climbed it?

**John**  No, lass, she never did.

**Sandra**  What a shame.

**John**  (*tapping his chest*) But she climbed it here with me today. (*He shakes off his sad mood*) Now isn't that the most sentimental rubbish you ever heard?

**Sandra**  Don't you dare say that. Don't you dare. I'll never be able to climb another hill without thinking of you and your Eileen.

**John**  Thank you, lass. That's a bonny thing to say. Ach, well. Now. I'm going to get going. (*He collects his things together*)

**Mark**  It's clearing. I can see Schiehallion. Look.

*Sandra moves to Mark and puts an arm around him*

**Sandra**  My God! It's beautiful! Look, John.

**John**  (*moving over to the others, putting on his rucksack*) The fairy hill of the Caledonians — the dead centre of Scotland. (*He winks at Sandra*) You'll enjoy climbing it.

**Sandra**  Are you sure about that?

**John**  I guarantee it. (*He laughs*) I'll be off. Hope to see you both again.

**Mark**  Bye.

**Sandra**  Yeh, see you, John. Thanks ... thanks for the soup.

**John**  No problem. I'll have some of yours, next time.

**Sandra**  If my dear husband remembers to bring it.

*John laughs, waves and exits, climbing down the hill*

*Sandra waves, then watches John's descent. She waves again*

Bye!

**Mark**  We can get going too. (*He collects his stuff together during the following*) Nice guy, that.

**Sandra**  (*following John with her eyes*) Very nice.

**Mark**  Imagine bumming his soup off him. Sandra, you have got some nerve. That was practically daylight robbery!

**Sandra**  Well, you'd never have spoken to him if it hadn't been for me.

**Mark**  I have to admit you're a great one for breaking the ice. "Till death do us part." Jesus! That was some gaffe. I was looking for a hole in the ground big enough to climb into.

**Sandra**  Don't worry, dear. I'll find you one on the way down. Anyway, John didn't seem to mind. In fact, I think he was happy to talk about his wife. Imagine, Mark. Poor woman. Dying twelve short of the whole complete set.

**Mark**  You make them sound like stamps.

**Sandra**  You're the collector. You're the one with the book full of ticks. Twelve short. Have many women climbed them all?

**Mark**  Oh, sure. One even did them in a single trip.

**Sandra**  What? Mm. That sounds a bit too athletic for me.

**Mark**  Don't tell me you're planning to do more?

**Sandra**  And why not?

**Mark**  Ten minutes ago, you were all set to hang up your boots. What about the quagmires, the bloody great boulders, the sheep, the midges, the flies, to say nothing of the damned mist?

**Sandra**  That was then. And in case you haven't noticed the damned mist has gone. (*She goes to the edge and looks down*) Look, look. There's John. By Christ, he can't half move!

*Mark joins Sandra*

He's going straight down.

**Mark**  Come on, then. Let's follow him. (*He puts on his rucksack*)

**Sandra**  What do you mean, "follow him"? We're not going that way.

**Mark**  (*puzzled*) Eh?

**Sandra**  I'm not leaving this mountain half done. We're going round the ridge to Stob na Whasits.

**Mark**  Are you kidding? I thought your feet ... ?

**Sandra**  Never mind my damned feet. I want to explore the whole character of this mountain. I want to achieve the total experience. I'm after an epiphany.

**John**  A what?

**Sandra**  The boy has no poetry in his soul.

**Mark**  Sandra. what the hell are you jibbering about? Are you sure
  you want to do the ridge?
**Sandra**  Sure, I'm sure. And I want to do it with a companion that
  I love. You do love me, don't you?
**Mark**  (*sighing*)  I suppose so.
**Sandra**  Well, don't overdo it! Let's go, beloved companion. Of
  course, if you're too tired ...
**Mark**  No ... no. Sandra, what on earth did that guy say to you?
**Sandra**  Never you mind. I'll tell you when we get home. Over a
  sandwich.

*Sandra links arms with Mark*

Come on, Sir Edmund. Show me some more of your pink rocks.

*They start to climb down together*

CURTAIN

# FURNITURE AND PROPERTY LIST

*Off stage:*     Rucksack. *In it:* flask of coffee, plasters, book, pencil, items of Sandra's clothing, small tin with inventory list, tube of Polos, squashed Mars bar (**Mark**)
Rucksack. *In it:* flask of soup, sandwiches (**John**)

*Personal:*      **John**: small stone

# LIGHTING PLOT

Practical fittings required: nil. One exterior scene throughout

*To open*: General exterior lighting

*No cues*

# EFFECTS PLOT

*No cues*

9 780573 121470